A magical performance

It's 1803, and violinist George Bridgetower is performing in Vienna, Austria. The composer of the piece, Ludwig van Beethoven, plays the piano. "The violin is a stringed instrument," says Pip. "When the strings are played, with a bow made of horsehair, the violin's wooden body makes the sound vibrate. Listen, he's playing short spiky notes, and smooth, long notes, too."

"I love the sound George is making!" says Sammy.

Can you clap the rhythm and join in with George?

Field of Dreams

"What a beautiful view!" Sighs Pip. "Look, there are poppies everywhere. And I can hear the sound of the cello through the gentle breeze."

"She's playing a famous piece by Edward Elgar," says Sammy. "The cello looks a lot like a violin, but it's much bigger—so she can make a deeper, richer sound. I could stay here all day!"

Close your eyes, and listen with the children. You could even lie on the floor!

A Starry Night

"What's this dreamy melody?" says Sammy. "It makes me feel as though I'm in a faraway land, gazing up at the night sky."

"That's because this flowing tune, by Cécile Charminade, is called Serenade to the Stars," says Pip.

"Flutes are made of silvery metal. This soft, whispery sound is making me feel sleepy."

Giraffe is playing the flute, too. Can you join in?

Evening in the City

It's the 1920s, in New York City. Evening lights sparkle, and the music of George Gershwin spills out from the concert halls into the city's cafés. Pip and Sammy are watching a clarinet player. "His instrument is made of wood, and has metal keys," says Sammy. "To make a sound, he has to blow."
"Look at his fingers move!" Says Pip. "I can hear deep, low notes and high, bendy ones too. I want to spin around and around."
Dance along with Pip as you listen!

Garden of Delights

The children find themselves in a colorful garden. A tune by Claude Debussy fills the air. "I can hear a saxophone!" says Pip. "It has a mouthpiece like a clarinet, but its body is made of metal, like a trumpet." "Debussy loved nature," says Sammy. "This piece makes me imagine fall leaves, dancing in the breeze."

Join the Dance!

It's 1902, and the children are in a café in Barcelona. Guitarist Francisco Tárrega is playing a piece called a Polka, which is a type of dance—and his family is watching. "He's playing so many notes at once," says Sammy. "Look, he's picking out the melody and strumming chords with one hand; with the other, he's shaping his fingers around the neck of the guitar. That's how he finds the notes."

Play along with Francisco, Pip and Sammy.

A Grand Performance

"What a room!" says Sammy. "It's 1868, and we're in a concert hall in London. Here's 15-year-old pianist Teresa Carreño, playing a piece she's written. She's from Venezuela."

"The piano has 88 keys," says Pip. "Each key is connected to a tiny hammer inside the piano, which strikes a string to make a sound. With ten fingers, pianists can play up to ten notes at once!"

Dance along with Pip, Sammy and Giraffe.

A Trumpet Fanfare

It's 1830, and a dramatic opera by Gioachino Rossini is being performed in Vienna, Austria. The story tells of a brave Swiss hero, William Tell, and his name is the title of the opera. "Look at me, I'm riding my horse across the mountains," says Pip. "And I'm playing my trumpet, a brass instrument made of tubes of curved metal. I have lots of energy—I'll never get tired with this tune galloping in my head!"

Can you sing the trumpet's tune?

Beats, Beats, Beats!

The children are in a jazz cafe in Paris. It's the 1960s. "Wow, listen to these drums!" says Pip. "In jazz, players take turns to play solos—and show everyone their amazing skills. The drummer is playing with lots of energy—I can hear the bass drum, the snare, and the crash of the cymbals. He's hitting them with sticks." *Throw your hands around, like you're playing imaginary drums!*

Listen to the Orchestra

Pip, Sammy and their toys are back at home. After their musical travels, they are getting ready for a concert. "We've had such fun," says Pip. "Can you name the instruments we've seen on our journey? I wonder if I can name them all." "I know, let's play one last tune together," says Sammy. "If we play a symphony, a piece of music written for a large orchestra, then everyone can join in."

Which instrument would you play in Pip and Sammy's orchestra?

Pip and Sammy have heard so much on their musical adventure, but your journey is just beginning!

As you've discovered, each instrument has a unique sound—from the soft, airy tone of the flute to the deep, rich sound of the cello. You might enjoy fast, energetic drums or slow, smooth clarinet melodies. There are so many different instruments and styles of playing to discover.

People have been making instruments since ancient times! The earliest ones were crafted from shells, bones, parts of plants, and animal skins. Today, instruments, like the ones you've seen in these pages, are usually made of wood, metal or combinations of many different materials. What an instrument is made from has a dramatic effect on the way it sounds. If you've enjoyed the instruments you've seen in these pages, there are others to discover, too. If you like the trumpet, you could listen to the trombone; if you're keen on the clarinet, you might like to hear the oboe.

Everyone can make music! It's such fun to learn. You don't have to own an instrument already—you can start by using your voice. For an accompaniment, pots, pans, and a wooden spoon make great drums, and you can make your own shaker from lentils, shells, or anything else that rattles, placed inside an empty container (like a milk carton). Many schools have instruments to play and even borrow. If you're lucky enough to own an instrument already, perhaps you could try out the different music styles you've heard in this book. In the meantime, always keep an ear out and...

LISTEN to the MUSIC!

Listen to the Music: The Instruments © 2024 Quarto Publishing plc. Illustrations © 2024. Text © Mary Richards

First published in 2024 by Wide Eyed Editions, an imprint of The Quarto Group. 100 Cummings Center, Suite 265D, Beverly, MA 01915 USA.
T +1 978-282-9590 F +1 978-283-2742 www.Quarto.com

The rights of Mary Richards to be identified as the author of this work and Khoa Le to be identified as the illustrator of this work have been asserted by them in accordance with the Copyright, Designs and Patents Act, 1988 (United Kingdom).

All rights reserved.

No part of this publication may be reproduced, stored in a retrieval system, or transmitted, in any form, or by any means, electrical, mechanical, photocopying, recording or otherwise without the prior written permission of the publisher or a licence permitting restricted copying.

Music licensed courtesy of Naxos Rights US Inc.
These clips have been edited for this book format.

A catalogue record for this book is available from the British Library.

ISBN 978-0-7112-9363-2

The illustrations were created with mixed media.
Set in Neutraface and Lust.

Editorial Director (Commissioning): Lucy Brownridge
Designer: Kathryn Davies and Lyli Feng
Art Director: Karissa Santos
Publisher: Georgia Buckthorn
Production Controller: Elizabeth Reardon
Sound Mixer: Matt Huxley

Manufactured in ShaoGuan, China SL062024
9 7 5 3 1 2 4 6 8